TRIBES of NATIVE AMERICA

Abenaki

edited by Marla Felkins Ryan
and Linda Schmittroth

BLACKBIRCH®
PRESS

THOMSON
★
GALE

San Diego • Detroit • New York • San Francisco • Cleveland
New Haven, Conn. • Waterville, Maine • London • Munich

For more information, contact
The Gale Group, Inc.
27500 Drake Rd.
Farmington Hills, MI 48331-3535
Or you can visit our Internet site at http://www.gale.com

LIBRARY OF CONGRESS CATALOGING-IN-PUBLICATION DATA

Abenaki / Marla Felkins Ryan, book editor ; Linda Schmittroth, book editor.
  v. cm. — (Tribes of Native America)
Includes bibliographical references and index.
Contents: Name — History — The English and the Iroquois — Abenaki tribes: the
Penobscot, Passamaquoddy, and Maliseet — Daily life — Customs.
  ISBN 1-56711-574-8 (alk. paper)
  1. Abenaki Indians—History—Juvenile literature. 2. Abenaki Indians—Social life
and customs—Juvenile literature. [1. Abenaki Indians. 2. Indians of North America—
Northeastern States.]
I. Ryan, Marla Felkins. II. Schmittroth, Linda. III. Series.

  E99.A13A24 2003
  974.004'973--dc21

                                                                      2003002624

Printed in United States
10 9 8 7 6 5 4 3 2 1

Table of Contents

ABENAKI

Name

Abenaki (pronounced *ah-buh-NAH-key*). The name means "people of the dawnlands." The Abenaki people called themselves Alnanbal, which means "men."

Where are the traditional Abenaki lands?

The Abenaki Indians were a group of many tribes that spoke the same language. They lived from the mid-1600s to about 1800. In 1670, the tribes formed the Abenaki Confederacy. The Abenaki were broken up into eastern and western groups. The eastern Abenaki lived in Maine and Canada. The western Abenaki lived in Vermont, New Hampshire, and parts of Massachusetts. By the late 1990s, most Abenaki lived on reservations in Maine or Canada.

A modern-day Abenaki boy prepares for a traditional dance performance.

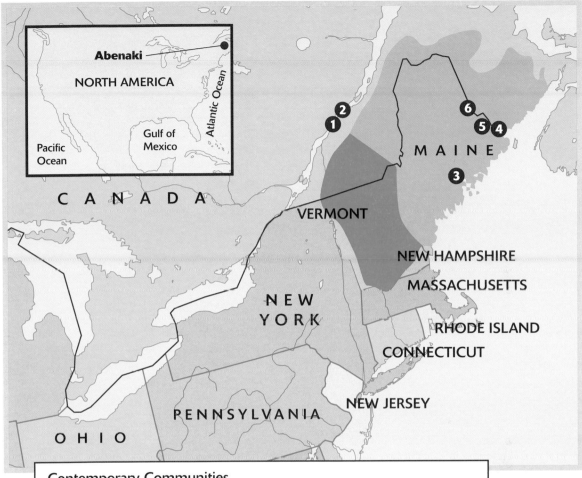

Contemporary Communities

Quebec
1. Odanak, Saint Francis Reserve
2. Abenakis de Wolinak

Maine
3. Penobscot Nation
4. Pleasant Point (Passamaquoddy) Reservation
5. Indian Township (Passamaquoddy) Reservation
6. Houlton Maliseet Reservation

Dark-shaded area: Traditional lands of western Abenaki in present-day Vermont, New Hampshire, and Massachusetts

Light-shaded area: Traditional lands of eastern Abenaki in present-day Maine, New Hampshire, New Brunswick, and Nova Scotia

What has happened to the population?

In 1524, there were about 40,000 Abenaki. Most were eastern Abenaki. In a 1990 population count by the U.S. Bureau of the Census, 1,549 people said they were Abenaki.

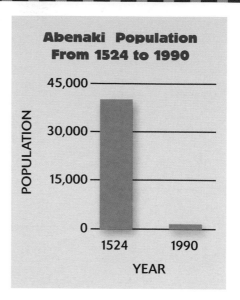

Abenaki Population From 1524 to 1990

Origins and group ties

The early ancestors of the Abenaki first arrived in North America about three thousand years ago. The eastern Abenaki group was made up of the Penobscot, Passamaquoddy, and Maliseet tribes. It also included the Androscoggin, Kennebec, Ossipee, and Pigwacket. The western Abenaki group was made up of the Sokoki, Cowasuck, and Missiquoi tribes. The eastern group was larger than the western branch.

Before Europeans came in the early 1600s, the Abenaki people had lived in peace. For thousands of years, they had hunted and fished in the forests and lakes of present-day Maine. From the 1600s to the 1800s, white settlers brought war, food shortages, and new illnesses to the Abenaki. During times of war, some Abenaki left their villages in New England and moved to Canada. While the Indians were away from their New England homes, white settlers took over Abenaki land. Some Abenaki stayed in Canada. They lived in peace there and kept many of their customs and traditions. The Abenaki in the United States tried to live in peace with the white settlers. Often, they were not able to do so.

Before Europeans arrived, the Abenaki lived in the forests of Maine.

HISTORY

Europeans arrive

In the early 1500s, people in Europe heard stories about a rich Native American city in Maine called Norumbega. The city was only a myth, but many explorers left Europe to find it. One of the first was Italian explorer Giovanni da Verrazano. He led a French expedition in 1524. At first, the Abenaki people did not trust the European newcomers. When the Europeans wanted to trade knives, axes, and cloth for fur pelts, the Abenaki decided to trade with them.

In 1604, French explorer Samuel de Champlain visited many Abenaki villages. He built a French fort on the Saint Croix River, on land that is part of present-day Maine. The English tried to build a colony on Abenaki land in 1607, but it lasted less than a year.

Samuel de Champlain built a French fort on Abenaki land in the early 1600s.

Abenaki relations with the French

For the next fifty years, the English and the French waged war for control of Abenaki lands. They fought over the land even though it belonged to the Indians. Soon, the Abenaki tribes began to fight each other. They competed over trade with the French. The French traded mostly with the Penobscot, which became the most powerful of the Abenaki tribes.

The Abenaki got along better with the French than with the English colonists. The French agreed to trade guns to the Abenaki. They also promised to protect the Abenaki from their longtime enemy, the Iroquois tribe.

The English and the Indians

The Abenaki rejected any attempts at friendship from the English. Between 1616 and 1619, deadly outbreaks of illness killed many Abenaki. The French told the Indians that the English caused these illnesses. The English became friends of the Iroquois tribe instead.

During the 1660s, a civil war took place in England. Many people fled the country for the New World. When they arrived, they began to settle on Abenaki lands. After a time of peace, King Philip's War erupted in 1675. A group of southern New

1929
Stock market crash begins the Great Depression

1941
Bombing at Pearl Harbor forces United States into WWII

1945
WWII ends

1950s
Reservations no longer controlled by federal government

1980
President Jimmy Carter signs a bill that grants the Passamaquoddy and Penobscot tribes $81 million to make up for the loss of their homelands

1982
Vermont Abenaki apply for recognition by the U.S. government. Ten years later, the Supreme Court rules against them

1989–1990
The National Museum of the American Indian Act and the Native American Grave Protection and Reparations Act bring about the return of burial remains to native tribes

In 1675, Chief Metacomet, also known as King Philip, led a war against the English colonists who had settled Abenaki land.

England tribes attacked English settlements on Indian lands. The Indians were led by the Wampanoag leader Metacomet, or King Philip. When the war was over, the colonists had killed nearly every member of the Wampanoag, Nipmuck, and Narragansett tribes. King Philip's death in July 1676 ended Native American battles in southern New England.

The French and Indian Wars begin

Between 1689 and 1763, Native Americans of the Northeast became caught up in a struggle between England and France. Both countries wanted to control North America. These battles are called the French and Indian Wars. There were outbreaks of war followed by times of peace. The final struggle in the United States between the English and French is called the French and Indian War (1754–1763).

King William's War

King William's War (1689–1697) was the first of the French and Indian Wars. Most Abenaki groups joined French troops to attack English towns in eastern New York, New Hampshire, and Maine. The English fought back. Many Abenaki fled to northern New England and Canada, where their French allies were based. England and France signed a peace agreement in 1697, but the Abenaki continued to fight. They were upset that more and more English colonists had taken over their lands. Worn out from war by 1699, the Abenaki signed an agreement not to take sides in future battles between England and France.

The Abenaki aided the French against the British during the French and Indian War (pictured).

This illustration shows Native Americans returning to their camp after taking English prisoners during the Deerfield Massacre.

Queen Anne's War

The peace between the English and the French did not last long. Queen Anne's War broke out in 1702. Most Abenaki stuck to the terms of their agreement not to take sides in the fight. Some Abenaki, however, joined the French in attacks on English towns.

The most famous raid of the war took place in February 1704 in Deerfield, Massachusetts. A large force of Abenaki and French led a sneak attack on the English at daybreak. They were successful, but the outnumbered Abenaki warriors suffered many losses. Weakened, the Abenaki were forced to trade more of their land to the French in exchange for safety in Canada.

Dummer's War

In the treaty that ended Queen Anne's War in 1713, the French gave the territory of Acadia (in present-day Nova Scotia) to England. Acadia was largely made up of Abenaki land. The Abenaki felt angry and betrayed that the French gave away their land. Many French people who lived in Acadia agreed with the Abenaki.

Supported by several French priests, the Abenaki decided to defend their land. In 1722, Dummer's War broke out. The great Abenaki warrior Grey Lock gained fame for his raids on the English. The conflict was bloody. The Abenaki met with defeat in 1727.

King George's War

Tribes in the Northeast lived in peace from 1727 to 1744. Years of war and outbreaks of smallpox had killed large numbers of Indians. Also, the Abenaki had become allies with other tribes and intermarried. The culture and lifestyle of these once fiercely independent groups had changed. Peace ended for the tribes with the outbreak of King George's War in 1744. Some Abenaki tribes once

Old Fort Number 4 was built during the French and Indian Wars to protect British settlers.

again joined the French to attack the English. They wanted to stop the English settlers before they invaded more Indian lands. The Indian raids ended in 1748. For a short time, the raids had forced the settlers to retreat southward.

Wars end but not troubles

The final battle was called the French and Indian War (1754–1763). It began well for the combined Abenaki and French forces. Later, the battle turned in favor of the English. In 1759, the Abenaki were dealt a serious blow. English major Robert Rogers and a group of soldiers burned the Abenaki village of Saint Francis, Quebec, to the ground.

The English set fire to and destroyed the village of the Saint Francis Abenaki in Quebec, Canada, during the final French and Indian War (1754-1763).

The English defeated the French army. England took control of Quebec and all of Canada. With the loss of their French allies, the Abenaki were forced to deal with the English alone. At the same time, English colonists invaded Abenaki lands in New England in great numbers.

Some Abenaki sided with the British during the Revolutionary War. Pictured here is a modern-day Abenaki dressed as his ancestors did in the war.

American Revolution splits Abenaki

After more than seventy years of war, starvation, and illness, the Abenaki had lost many members. Their troubles were not over. The Abenaki were forced to endure more warfare when they were drawn into the American Revolution in 1776. The various Abenaki bands did not agree on which side to support in the revolution. Many of the Saint Francis Abenaki in Quebec supported the British. The Penobscot, Passamaquoddy, Maliseet, and Micmac tribes fought with the colonists under the command of General George Washington. The colonists promised the Abenaki land in exchange for their support. For the most part, these promises were later broken.

Abenaki migrate north

When the United States was formed in 1783, the Abenaki's help in the victory was quickly forgotten. White-owned lumber companies took over Abenaki lands and cut down trees. Then, the United States and Canada drew borderlines through Abenaki lands and broke up the tribe's territory. The Indians could not get help from state governments. On five separate times in the 1800s, the state of Vermont refused to give land to the Abenaki.

At the beginning of the 19th century, Abenaki continued to move north into Canada. They wanted to escape from the ever-growing number of American settlers. In 1805, the British government set aside land near Saint Francis, Quebec, for the flood of Abenaki settlers.

U.S. Abenaki try to fit in

Some Abenaki stayed behind in the United States. To survive, they adopted the ways of the whites. They also learned to speak English. Abenaki customs were soon lost. White loggers destroyed the lands

Logging by whites in the 1800s destroyed Abenaki forests.

where the Abenaki had always hunted, fished, and trapped. They were no longer able to support themselves this way. Many Abenaki began to make and sell baskets and other crafts to survive.

In New England, the Passamaquoddy and Penobscot tribes lived on their original homeland. In 1794, they were forced to give up more than a million acres of land. By 1820, the Abenaki owned only a few thousand acres. They were confined to two separate villages by 1850.

Abenaki in the 20th century

In the late 1920s and the 1930s, the Abenaki in the United States were helped by programs started by President Franklin D. Roosevelt (1882–1945). He called the Native American the "forgotten man." Roosevelt's programs provided food and jobs for people in the United States who suffered hardships.

President Franklin D. Roosevelt (left) started programs to aid Native Americans.

During Roosevelt's presidency, government policies toward Native Americans changed. The new goal was to preserve ancient Indian culture.

This positive trend was soon reversed. Some Abenaki joined other Native Americans to fight in World War II (1939–1945). After the war, Native American soldiers returned home to find that the U.S. government's policies had changed back. Once again, the government wanted Indians to blend into mainstream white society.

Abenaki win rights

In the 1950s, American Abenaki voiced their anger at government policies that had taken away most of their land. These policies had also taken away their right to fish on their lands. In the 1960s, the Abenaki began to demand that they be given back their rights as a tribe.

In 1980, President Jimmy Carter signed a bill that settled claims by two Abenaki tribes from Maine, the Passamaquoddy and the Penobscot.

Abenaki beliefs included a hero named Glooskap.

In 1980, the U.S. government gave the Passamaquoddy and Penobscot tribes $81 million to make up for the earlier loss of their homelands. Most of the money was used to buy 300,000 acres of their former land.

Religion

The Abenaki were very religious. They believed that the earth had always existed. They called it "Grandmother." They also believed that a being called the Owner had created people, animals, and natural things such as rocks and trees. Their hero, Glooskap, who had created himself, could make life good or bad for the people.

The spiritual leaders of the Abenaki were healers called shamans (pronounced *SHAH-munz* or *SHAY-munz*). Shamans asked the spirits to help them heal the sick and solve problems.

During the 16th and 17th centuries, French Catholic missionaries tried to convert the Abenaki to Christianity. The priests gained the trust of many Abenaki. In time, Roman Catholic churches and cemeteries became important parts of many Abenaki villages.

Traditionally, the sachem, or chief, guided the Abenaki people. Homer St. Francis, pictured here in 1995, served several terms as chief during the 1970s, 1980s, and 1990s.

Government

When the Europeans arrived in the Northeast, the different Abenaki groups did not have a strong form of government. Major decisions were made by all the adult members of a tribe. A well-respected person called a sachem (pronounced *SAY-chem*) or chief guided the people. A sachem might direct a war or represent the people in meetings with other tribes. Even after the Abenaki Confederacy was formed in 1670, French military officers complained that Abenaki leaders were not able to control their warriors.

Economy

The Abenaki were hunter-gatherers who also fished. After Europeans arrived on their lands, trade became more important. In Europe, many wealthy people lived in drafty houses and castles. They would pay large sums of money for furs to keep themselves warm in winter. The Abenaki and other tribes supplied European traders, especially the French, with fur pelts. By the mid-1660s, the fur trade had slowed down because the animals had been overhunted. The British allowed the Abenaki to buy European goods on credit and use their land as a guarantee of payment. This meant that whites could take native American land if the Indians did not repay the loan on time. After a while, the British refused to be repaid in animal skins and only accepted Abenaki land.

The Abenaki, like other Native American tribes, traded animal skins to Europeans. The skins were often stretched on frames.

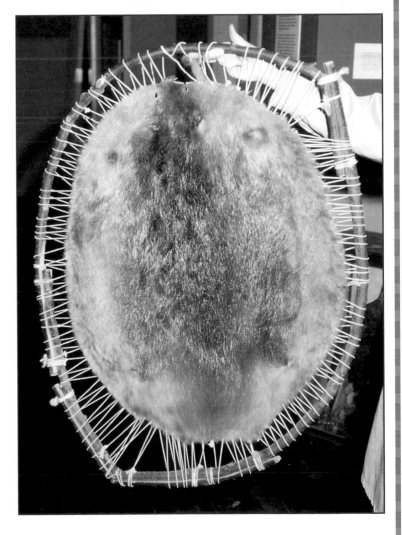

DAILY LIFE

Families

A typical Abenaki family had a father, mother, their children, grandparents, aunts, uncles, and cousins. Several related families lived together in the same large house, but each family had its own living space and fire. Family members shared food and possessions. In the summer, the family groups lived on hunting lands that were inherited through the fathers. Abenaki villages rarely had more than one hundred people.

The Abenaki lived in fairly small, close-knit communities.

Buildings

Most Abenaki buildings were made from the bark of birch trees. Western Abenaki families lived together in longhouses. When food became scarce in the winter, families sometimes moved into wigwams. Shaped like a cone, the wigwam was covered with mats made from the bark of elm trees. Wigwams were not as sturdy as longhouses, but they could be moved easily while a family hunted game animals.

The eastern Abenaki built two different kinds of homes. Some houses were shaped like domes. Other houses were square and had roofs shaped like pyramids.

Clothing

The Abenaki made most of their clothing from deerskin. In warm weather, men wore breechcloths. These garments had front and back flaps that hung from the waist. Women

Western Abenaki lived in longhouses. When they needed to hunt, they often moved to wigwams, which were more portable.

The Abenaki made much of their clothing, such as these moccasins, from deerskin.

wore wraparound knee-length skirts. In the cold winter months, the Abenaki wore fur robes with hoods. They also wore moccasins that were lined with rabbit fur.

Both men and women wore their hair long. Women sometimes wore braids. They often wore necklaces decorated with shells.

Food

The Abenaki hunted and fished for most of their food. In the spring, they fished from their canoes for salmon, sturgeon, and eels. They used nets, three-pronged spears, and fencelike traps called weirs to catch fish.

During the summer, Abenaki who lived on the coast harvested the ocean for fish, shellfish, and sea mammals. In the fall, the Abenaki used bows and arrows to hunt both large and small game. Some Abenaki fished on frozen ponds during the winter. They wore snowshoes made from wood and leather to hunt deer, bear, and otter in the cold weather.

The Abenaki grew crops such as corn, beans, squash, and tobacco along the rivers. In areas where the soil was less rich, the Abenaki used fish as fertilizer. Every February the western Abenaki collected maple sap, which they boiled to make syrup.

Women gathered nuts and berries to eat raw or bake into breads. They also planted crops such as beans, corn, and squash.

Traps were used to catch fish.

Corn was a favorite crop of the Abenaki who lived along rivers.

Education

Abenaki children were often raised by their grandparents, aunts, or uncles. Boys were taught the skills needed to hunt or wage war. They began to practice with a bow and arrow at a very young age. By age twelve, they could hunt with the men of the family. Girls were taught how to weave baskets, grow crops, and sew clothing. They also learned how to care for younger children.

Healing practices

Healers, or shamans, took care of sick people in Abenaki villages. Most shamans were men. They used herbs, teas, and ointments to cure the sick or wounded. When herbs did not cure a person, a

The Abenaki shaped birch bark into boxes (top) and other useful and decorative objects such as canoes (below).

shaman used magic to treat an illness. The shaman might try to dance an illness away. If the sick person was near death, villagers let the person starve to bring death more quickly. This practice was considered kind.

Arts

The Abenaki made decorative objects from the bark of white birch trees. The tree bark was shaped into baskets, boxes, and canoes. Many of the objects were not only useful but works of art.

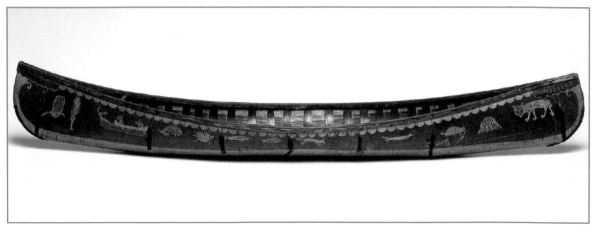

CUSTOMS

Games and festivities

Games have always been an important part of Abenaki culture. Boys began to race when they were small. Handball and lacrosse were popular games for the Abenaki.

The Abenaki liked to sing and tell stories as they did their daily chores. They also enjoyed riddles and word games. They danced and sang at most social events, such as marriages, funerals, and the first corn harvest of the year.

Dances were part of most Abenaki social events.

Abenaki warriors painted their faces for battle.

War and hunting rituals

When conflicts broke out with other peoples, the Abenaki war chief would stand before the tribe with a red club in his hands. He would ask for volunteers to unite for the fight. Then, the men feasted and danced well into the night. Before the battle, warriors painted their faces red and drew pictures of past battle victories on their bodies.

Puberty

Around the time of puberty, an Abenaki boy went on a vision quest. Alone in the woods, he fasted for many days. Then, he waited for the guardian spirit who would guide him through life to appear. Males were considered adults by age fifteen. Some girls also went on vision quests.

Marriage

When a young man wanted to marry, he sent gifts to his intended bride to entice her into marriage. If she refused the gifts, it meant that she rejected the proposal. If she and her parents agreed, the couple lived together for a trial period. They were supervised by chaperones and had to follow strict rules.

Marriages became official when the groom's family accepted gifts offered by the bride's family. A wedding celebration was held. For western Abenaki, new couples lived with the husband's family after marriage. If the bride's family were wealthier, the couple lived with them. Eastern Abenaki newlyweds usually lived with the bride's family. Some chiefs of the eastern Abenaki were allowed to have many wives.

Abenaki women had a large say in deciding whom they married. In this 1921 photo, the Penobscot chief (right) talks with his wife.

Weapons were buried with their owners. The Abenaki believed that the deceased would be able to use them in the afterlife.

Funerals

The bodies of dead Abenaki were dressed in their finest clothing, wrapped in birch bark, and tied with a cord. They were buried quickly so that their spirits would not linger over the village. Food was put in the grave for the deceased person's journey to the other world. Also in the grave were weapons, tools, and personal items to use in the afterlife.

Current tribal issues

In the 1980s, the Abenaki Indians of Vermont fought in court for the right to hunt, fish, and travel on their traditional lands. In 1992, the Vermont Supreme Court ruled that all of these Abenaki rights had ended. The Vermont Abenaki continued to fight. In the late 1990s, the General Assembly of Vermont recognized the tribal status of the Abenaki people. The tribe's next goal is to gain recognition by the U.S. government. When the federal government recognizes a group of Native Americans as an Indian tribe, they are granted the right to hunt and fish on their homeland. The tribe also receives better health care and educational benefits.

Notable people

Joseph E. Bruchac III, Ph.D. (1942–), is an author and poet whose works reflect his Native American

Samoset (center) worked for peace between the Pilgrims and Native Americans in the 17th century.

heritage. His books have won many awards. He has also written many stories for children.

A Penobscot named Louis Francis Sockalexis (1871–1913) was the first Native American to play professional baseball. He was an outstanding hitter for the Cleveland Spiders. In 1915, the Cleveland team was renamed the Indians in his honor. (In the 1980s and 1990s, many Native Americans protested the use of Indian names in sports as demeaning.)

Samoset (1590–1653) was a chief who lived on an island off the coast of present-day Maine. He served as a go-between for the Pilgrims and Native American groups. Samoset helped to create the first peace agreement between whites and the Wampanoag tribe.

For more information

Landau, Elaine. *The Abenaki.* New York: Franklin Watts, 1996.

Prins, Harald E. "Abenaki," in *American Indians.* Vol. 1. Edited by Harvey Markowitz. Pasadena, CA: Salem Press, 1995.

Glossary

Lacrosse a Native American game played with a ball and long poles with webbed pouches

Longhouse a long building in which several Native American families lived together

Sachem chief

Shaman a Native American priest who used magic to heal people and see the future

Treaty an agreement between two or more parties

Vision quest a Native American child's search for his or her guardian spirit

Weir a trap used for fishing

Wigwam a Native American hut made of bark and hides

Index